MACMILLAN READERS

INTERMEDIATE LEVEL

GEOFFREY MATTHEWS

The Space Invaders

MACMILLAN

MACMILLAN READERS

INTERMEDIATE LEVEL

Founding Editor: John Milne

The Macmillan Readers provide a choice of enjoyable reading materials for learners of English. The series is published at six levels – Starter, Beginner, Elementary, Pre-intermediate, Intermediate and Upper.

Level control
Information, structure and vocabulary are controlled to suit the students' ability at each level.

The number of words at each level:

Starter	about 300 basic words
Beginner	about 600 basic words
Elementary	about 1100 basic words
Pre-intermediate	about 1400 basic words
Intermediate	about 1600 basic words
Upper	about 2200 basic words

Vocabulary
Some difficult words and phrases in this book are important for understanding the story. Some of these words are explained in the story and some are shown in the pictures. From Pre-intermediate level upwards, words are marked with a number like this: …[3]. These words are explained in the Glossary at the end of the book.

Contents

1

'I am Omega'

Varon pushed his way through the thick, wet grass of the swamp[1]. Behind him, he heard the sound of loud voices. He tried to go faster, but the thick grass held him back. He had to push his way through it step by step. Varon had come about three kilometres from the Zeron strongroom[2] and was very tired.

The first part of Varon's plan[3] had been successful. He had got into the strongroom deep under the ground – he had found the crystal[4] – and he had got out again. He had succeeded in stealing one of the most valuable crystals in the Universe[5]. And no one had seen him.

But the second part of his plan had gone completely wrong. The guards on the planet Zeron had found his spaceship. Varon had been told that only the strongroom on Zeron was guarded. But now he knew that was wrong. There were guards all over the planet. The guards had been waiting for him when he got back to the spaceship. And now they were chasing him and there was no way he could escape.

Varon pushed his way through the grass and fell into a pool of dirty, green water. The shouts were coming closer. He had to keep moving.

Varon pulled himself slowly to his feet. His face, hands and overalls[6] were covered in thick green mud. Varon wiped his hands on his overalls and felt in his pocket. The small, square box was still there. And in the box, there was the Zeron crystal. The crystal would make him rich – very, very rich. But first, he had to get back inside his ship. There was no other way he could escape from Zeron.

He now moved out of the long, thick grass. He was standing on harder, drier ground. There were some thick bushes in front of him. Behind him, there was the swamp and the guards who were chasing him. Varon hurried towards the thick bushes.

'I must get back to the spaceship,' Varon thought. 'I'll have to find some way of tricking[7] the guards. I can't escape from Zeron if I can't get back to the spaceship.'

Varon took two steps forward into the bushes. Suddenly he stopped. He knew he was not alone. He dropped down on one knee. There was somebody near him. His hand reached for the laser gun[8] on his belt.

'Do not touch your weapon,' said a soft voice.

The voice spoke from behind a bush. Varon turned towards the voice and pulled his gun from his belt. He pointed the laser gun at the bush and pressed the trigger[9]. Nothing happened. Varon pressed the trigger again. Again, nothing happened.

The quiet voice spoke once more. 'Your gun cannot be used. Put it back in your belt. You will not be harmed[10].'

Varon lowered his hand, but did not put the gun back in his belt. He rose slowly and took a step towards the bush.

'You are not permitted[11] to move any nearer,' said the soft, quiet voice. It was a strange voice – neither friendly nor unfriendly.

Varon raised his foot to take another step towards the bush. But he could not move his leg forward. He tried and tried to move his leg, but it would not move. He could move backwards, but he could not go nearer the bush.

'Who are you?' Varon asked. 'What do you want from me?'

'I want to help you, Stefan Varon,' said the voice.

'You know my name!' said Varon in surprise. No one on Zeron knew him.

'Yes, I know your name. And I know what you do. And where you come from. And why you are here. I know every thing. I am Omega.'

The leaves of the bush were moved slowly to one side. A tall figure stood in front of Varon. The figure was made of metal. Its face was neither friendly nor unfriendly. It did not have a nose, mouth, eyes and ears like a human. It was a robot[12]!

Varon was very surprised. He knew that the guards on Zeron did not use robots. He knew there were no robots on Zeron. Or was he wrong again? A robot was standing here in front of him.

'What do you want from me?' Varon asked once again.

The robot did not reply. It seemed to be listening to something. Its head moved round to the right. Varon heard the voices of the Zeron guards.

'He's over there,' a voice shouted. 'Near those bushes!'

Varon turned to the left and began to run. Omega raised one arm and pointed it at Varon. A bright, red light came from the metal arm and covered Varon's body. The red light quickly faded[13]. When the Zeron guards reached the bushes, they found nothing. Varon and Omega had disappeared.

———

A tall figure stood in front of Varon. It was a robot!

2

On the Spaceship

Varon opened his eyes and looked around. He was lying on a metal bunk[14] in a small room. The bunk was fixed to a metal wall.

'The Zeron guards have caught me,' he thought. 'I am in prison.'

There was a small screen in the metal wall opposite the bunk. Varon got up and pressed a switch. The screen lit up and a picture appeared. Outside there were thousands and thousands of stars and planets. The biggest was a large circle of bright, yellow light. Varon had seen the same yellow light when he was coming towards Zeron in his spaceship. Now he was looking at the planet Zeron from space. A short time ago, he had been standing in a swamp on its surface.

'I'm in a spaceship,' Varon said to himself. 'And it's not my spaceship. But how did I get here?'

Then he remembered the Zeron guards who had been chasing him. And he remembered Omega.

'The robot has teleported[15] me here,' he said to himself. 'But what about the Zeron crystal? Have I still got it?'

Quickly he felt in his pocket for the small box. It was still there. He opened the box and looked at the red crystal lying inside. He was lucky. No one had searched his pockets. No one had taken his precious[16] crystal.

Varon looked around the room for a hiding place. There was no furniture – only the metal walls and the metal bunk. There was the small visual display screen[17] in one wall and

above the bunk there was a small air vent[18]. The air vent was covered with a metal grille[19].

Varon took a small metal tool from his pocket. He pointed the instrument at the edge of the grille and pressed a button. There was a humming[20] noise. Varon pointed the tool at the grille and moved his arm round slowly in a circle. After a few seconds, he reached up and carefully lifted the grille away from the air vent.

He took the box with the crystal in it from his pocket and placed it carefully inside the vent. He put the grille back in place. He used the instrument again. In a few seconds, the grille was firmly fixed back to the wall.

There was no door in the room. But this did not trouble Varon. He pointed the metal tool at the wall between the visual display screen and the bunk. He pressed the button. Nothing happened. Then he turned round and pointed at the other wall. He pressed the button again and this time there was a soft sliding noise. Part of the wall slid to one side. Varon had opened the door.

The corridor outside the room was long and dark, but there was a light at one end. Very quietly, Varon moved down the corridor towards the light. The light was coming from an open door. Varon stopped at the side of the door and carefully looked inside. It was the control room[21] of the spaceship.

There was someone standing inside, near the open door. Quickly, Varon moved back and stood against the metal wall of the corridor.

A woman's voice said. 'It was a mistake to bring him up here to the ship.'

'Mistakes are made by humans. I do not make mistakes,' said a quiet voice. Varon knew the voice immediately. It was Omega's voice.

'You have made a mistake,' the woman repeated angrily. She said each word sharply and coldly.

Varon very slowly moved back towards the open door. He looked carefully into the control room. He saw Omega standing in front of the controls of the spaceship. The woman was standing looking at Omega angrily. She was young, about twenty-five, and she had long, bright red hair.

'You must send this man back to Zeron immediately,' said the woman.

'I cannot do harm to a human being,' Omega replied quietly. 'If I send the man back to Zeron, he will be killed by the guards. I cannot send him back.'

Varon smiled. He did not want to go back to Zeron.

'But you must obey[22] my orders,' said the woman.

'That is correct,' said Omega.

10

'Then I order you to send this man back to Zeron.'

Omega stood quietly at the controls of the spaceship. He did not do anything.

'Obey my order immediately!' shouted the woman. 'Teleport this man back to Zeron.'

'I do not understand your order,' said Omega quietly.

'It is a simple order,' said the woman angrily. 'Send him back to Zeron.'

The woman now turned towards the robot. Varon could see she was very angry. Her eyes were bright and hard. She had raised her arms and her hands were tightly closed.

'Your order is not simple. It does not make sense. I cannot obey it.' Omega's voice was quiet and soft.

'Why not?'

'Varon is a human being. That is correct?' said Omega.

The woman agreed.

'I cannot harm a human being. If I send him back to Zeron, he will die. Therefore I cannot send him back. I cannot obey your order.'

'Good,' thought Varon to himself. He did not want to go back to Zeron to die. But he did want to go back to Earth. And this spaceship could take him there. He had to find a way to get control of the spaceship. Varon started to move back away from the open door.

'Stay where you are,' said a man's voice behind him. 'Do not move.'

Varon felt cold metal touch the back of his neck. He knew that the man was pointing a laser gun at his head. He stood very still.

Varon felt cold metal touch the back of his neck.

3

Three Thieves

Raise your hands,' said the man behind Varon, 'and walk slowly into the control room.'

Varon obeyed the man's order.

'Now sit down on that seat,' said the voice. 'And do it slowly.'

Varon stopped in front of the seat. He slowly turned round and sat down. Now Varon could see the man. He was tall and his black hair was cut short.

'What are you doing, Garth?' asked the woman. 'Why have you brought that man in here?'

Garth stood back against the wall. He held his laser gun loosely. But it was pointing straight at Varon's head. Varon knew that Garth could kill him easily and that he would enjoy doing it.

'I did not bring him here, Miranda,' Garth replied. 'I found him standing outside the door. He was listening to you and Omega.'

'But how did he get out of the room?' asked Miranda. 'I closed and locked the door. No one can open the door from the inside.'

'I can get out of any room if I have the right tool,' said Varon. He smiled at the woman. She looked beautiful, but she did not smile back at him.

'You're a fool, Miranda,' said Garth. 'You did not search him. Do it now.'

Miranda walked behind the seat Varon was sitting on. She

leant forward and searched his pockets. She took out the metal tool and handed it to Garth. Garth looked at it carefully.

'You're right,' Garth said to Varon with a cold smile. 'You can get out of any room if you have a tool like this. It's a sonic key[23]. It can open almost anything. Now, why do you need a tool like this?'

'For my work,' replied Varon.

'What is your work?' asked Garth. He was still smiling but it was not a friendly smile.

Varon did not reply. Garth spoke to Omega.

'Who is this man?' he ordered sharply. 'Tell me what he was doing on the planet Zeron.'

Omega was standing quietly at the controls of the space-ship. He did not reply for a few seconds. Then he spoke.

'Varon is a thief. The Zeron guards were chasing him,'

14

came the quiet reply.

'Why were the guards chasing you?' Garth asked Varon.

'Your friend knows everything,' replied Varon. 'Ask him.'

'Omega is not a friend of ours,' said Miranda. 'He is a robot.'

'I know that,' said Varon. 'But a robot can still be a friend. He must be a friend. He's controlling your spaceship.'

'This is not their spaceship,' said Omega. 'And I am not their friend.'

'Omega is right as usual,' said Garth, with a sharp laugh. 'The owner of this ship was his friend. Unfortunately, we had to leave him on Earth when we stole the ship.'

'You did not leave him on Earth,' said Omega in his quiet voice. 'You killed my master when you stole this spaceship.'

'And we found out how to control you,' said Garth in a cold, hard voice. 'Now you must obey our orders. We are your masters.'

Omega was silent.

'That's interesting,' Varon thought to himself. 'If I can learn how to control Omega, I can make him fly the ship back to Earth. I must watch the robot carefully.'

Varon looked at Garth and Miranda. The woman was beautiful, but her eyes were hard and cruel.

'Why did you steal this spaceship?' asked Varon.

'Because we needed it,' replied Miranda. 'We had to leave Earth quickly. We were being chased by the Earth police.'

'Why were they chasing you?' asked Varon. He was interested now.

'Because we succeeded in stealing the most valuable thing on Earth,' Miranda said quickly. Her eyes were bright with joy.

Varon laughed loudly. 'Then you are both the same as me.

I am a thief too. We are three thieves together.'

'We are not the same as you,' said Miranda coldly. 'We are successful thieves. We only steal things of great value. What can you steal on Zeron? It is a poor planet. There is nothing to steal on Zeron. Everyone knows that.'

'Yes, Varon,' said Garth, 'we are not the same as you. We are successful thieves.' They both laughed.

'They are very stupid,' thought Varon to himself. 'They do not know the secret of Zeron. They do not know that a Zeron crystal is the most valuable thing in this Universe.'

Then Omega spoke quietly. He stood at the controls of the spaceship with his back towards the three humans. 'Varon is exactly like you.'

Garth stopped laughing. He turned sharply towards the metal figure. 'You are wrong, Omega.'

'I am never wrong,' was Omega's reply. 'And I can prove that Varon is the same as you.'

'I hope he isn't going to tell them about the Zeron crystals,' Varon thought to himself.

'Tell Varon why you and Miranda left Earth,' Omega said.

'You say you know everything,' said Garth to Omega in a cold voice, 'you tell him why we left Earth.'

'They stole the newest and most powerful computer[24] on Earth,' said Omega in a quiet voice. 'They stole it. But the Earth police discovered that they were the thieves. They had to escape and so they stole this spaceship.'

'The most powerful computer on Earth?' said Varon. 'Then you are rich – very rich.'

'They are not rich yet,' continued Omega. 'They had to hide the computer on Earth. It is still on Earth.'

'So Garth and Miranda stole the computer but they have

not sold it yet,' said Varon with a laugh.

'The computer is hidden safely,' said Miranda angrily. 'No one can ever find it. It will be there when we get back to Earth.'

'There are many people who want this powerful computer,' said Garth. 'And when we sell it we will be rich. We will be the richest people on Earth.'

For the first time Omega turned away from the controls. He looked at Garth and Miranda.

'Yes, you will both be rich when you get back to Earth,' Omega said. 'But first you must get back there. And that is why you are both the same as Varon. He too is rich – much richer than both of you. But he too must get back to Earth.'

Miranda and Garth looked at Varon with great interest. He was richer than they were. What did he have which made him so rich?

4

'You Need Varon's Help'

There was silence on the spaceship. Omega was standing quietly at the controls again. Varon was thinking about how he could learn to control Omega. Miranda and Garth were thinking about what Omega had told them. Varon was richer than both of them.

Miranda was the first to speak.

'So we all want to go back to Earth,' she said. 'Then let's go there. Omega, take us back to Earth, now.'

Omega pushed switches on the control panel. A low noise filled the room.

'Stop,' said Garth sharply. 'Stop, Omega. We cannot go back to Earth yet.'

Omega pulled back the switches and the noise faded away.

'You are stupid, Miranda,' said Garth. 'We have travelled millions of kilometres through space. We have been running and hiding from everyone for a long time now. But we can't go back to Earth yet. First, we must make sure that our plan has worked.'

'Plan?' asked Varon. 'What's your plan?'

'It's simple,' replied Garth. 'When we stole the computer, we knew that the Earth police were following us. So we stole this spaceship – the fastest spaceship that has ever been built.'

'The fastest and most powerful,' added Omega.

'When we left Earth, we flew towards the Moon,' continued Garth. 'The police ships were far behind. We fired a small missile[25] at the surface of the Moon. By the time it exploded, we were thousands of kilometres away.'

'But what was the plan?' asked Varon.

'The police saw the missile explode,' explained Garth. 'We hope they will believe that this ship crashed on the Moon. Then they will think we are dead and they will forget about us.'

'A clever plan,' said Varon. 'But has it worked?'

'It's time to find out,' said Miranda. 'We have been hiding for long enough. Omega, find out if our plan has worked.'

Omega moved to one side of the control panel. He stood in front of a large, white screen. He placed his arms on the controls at each side of the screen. Bright lights, red and green and blue, flashed across the screen. There was a humming noise.

After a few moments, the bright lights faded away and the noise stopped. There was silence. Omega took his arms away from the control panel. He turned slowly towards Garth and Miranda.

'The Earth police have stopped looking for you,' he said quietly. 'They believe that this ship crashed on the Moon. They think that the ship was completely destroyed[26] and that both of you are dead.'

Miranda laughed with joy.

'The plan has worked,' she cried excitedly. 'Now we can go back to Earth and get the computer.'

19

'But what about him?' asked Garth, pointing at Varon.

'Take me back to Earth with you,' said Varon. 'I have some business there.'

'I am sure you have business there,' said Garth. 'But I think you've forgotten something.'

'What's that?' asked Varon.

'You are the only person who knows that we are still alive,' answered Garth. 'You are the only person who knows we have this ship. If we take you back to Earth, you could tell the police. They will pay a big reward[27].'

'A big reward,' said Varon with a laugh. 'Haven't you forgotten something?'

'Tell me what I have forgotten.'

'You have forgotten what Omega has told you,' replied Varon. 'When I get back to Earth, I will be richer than both of you. I don't need any reward from the police.'

'You won't be richer than us,' said Garth in a harsh voice. 'You will never get back to Earth. I am going to kill you now.'

Garth pointed his laser gun at Varon's head.

'Don't kill him,' said Miranda suddenly. Her eyes were shining with greed. 'First, find out what he has got. Why will he be richer than both of us?'

'I don't believe Omega,' said Garth. 'It's impossible. There's nothing to steal on Zeron.'

Garth put his fingers to the trigger of the gun. But he could not close his fingers. Omega's arm was pointing at Garth.

'You must not kill this man,' said Omega. 'You must ask him to help you. You need his help.'

'Help?' asked Miranda sharply. 'What help?'

'If Varon does not help you, you will never get back to Earth!'

5

Under Attack

'What do you mean?' asked Garth. 'Why do we need help from Varon?'

Omega did not reply. Suddenly there was a loud noise in the control room. Omega turned to the controls. Red lights were flashing on the control panel and the noise was growing louder.

The voice of the spaceship's warning system[28] suddenly sounded in the control room.

'*Emergency – emergency. We are under attack. Hostile[29] ships are approaching. We are under attack. Emergency – emergency.*'

'It's the Zeron guards,' said Omega. 'They have found us here above their planet. They are looking for Varon.'

'Omega, I order you to teleport Varon back to Zeron,' said Garth. 'The guards don't know Miranda and I are in this ship. They want Varon.'

'No, don't do anything, Omega,' said Miranda angrily. 'Varon is rich. We must find out where his wealth is.'

'Omega,' shouted Garth, 'I order you to take him back!'

'Too late,' said Omega quietly. 'The ship is in danger. We must be away from here in fifteen seconds. Prepare for hyper-flight[30]. Humans must go to the safety room.'

The voice of the warning system sounded again, '*Hostile ships in attack range[31] in fourteen seconds . . . thirteen seconds . . .*'

A door slid open on one side of the control room. Garth and Miranda ran towards the door. Varon followed quickly. They went into a small room with metal walls. It was like the room in which Varon had been a prisoner. But there were many metal bunks.

'. . . *eight seconds* . . .'

Garth pressed a switch in the wall. A tray slid out of the wall. There were some large blue capsules on the tray. Garth and Miranda each swallowed a blue capsule. Varon swallowed a blue capsule too.

'. . . *five seconds* . . .'

The three humans lay down on the bunks.

'. . . *two seconds* . . .'

The door of the safety room closed. They were now shut tightly in the room. Varon felt sleepy. A second later, the three of them were unconscious[32].

Omega was now part of the controls of the spaceship. He had placed his arms on the control panel. He was a powerful computer controlling the ship.

The noises became much louder and the lights in the control room faded. The control room shook violently. But Omega felt nothing. And the three humans felt nothing. They were lying unconscious on the bunks in the safety room.

Omega increased the power to the controls. The spaceship began to move into hyper-flight. It was the fastest ship that had ever been built. The lights in the control room went out. The noise stopped. There was complete blackness and silence in the control room. They were travelling out into space faster than the speed of light.

In a few seconds, they had left the planet Zeron far behind them. The spaceships of the Zeron guards could not follow them.

Slowly the lights in the control room came on again. There were no noises and no flashing lights. Omega moved his arms from the control panel.

'What do I do now?' Omega asked himself. 'If I do not wake them up, they will lie in the safety room for ever. But I am a robot. I am not free. I cannot harm a human being. I cannot leave them there.'

Omega pressed a switch on the control panel. The three humans woke up. The door of the safety room slid quietly open. In a few seconds, they were back in the control room with Omega.

'What is our position?' asked Garth.

'We have escaped from the Zeron guards,' replied Omega. 'Their spaceships could not follow us.'

'Good,' said Miranda. 'Now we can get back to Earth. We do not need to hide any longer.'

'It is too late to go back to Earth now,' said Omega quietly.

'Too late?' asked Garth in surprise. 'What do you mean?'

'I will explain,' replied Omega. 'Since we left Earth, we have travelled many millions of kilometres. When we reached Zeron, our power banks[33] were almost empty. I took this ship to Zeron because I knew the secret of the planet. There is a source of power[34] on Zeron. But we had to escape from the Zeron guards. The escape used all the power we had left.'

'No power left!' said Garth. 'But that's impossible. What about power for the life support systems[35]?'

'You have exactly forty minutes left,' answered Omega. 'Then the life support systems will fail.'

'And we will all die,' said Varon.

'I will not die,' said Omega. 'But I will be left here in this ship for ever.'

'But you said Varon could help us,' Miranda said sharply to Omega. 'How can he help us?'

'Varon stole a crystal from Zeron,' replied Omega. 'Zeron crystals are the strongest source of power that has yet been discovered. One Zeron crystal in our power banks and we can go anywhere we want.'

Garth and Miranda turned towards Varon. Garth took his laser gun from his belt.

'Where is this crystal?' he asked Varon.

6

'Steal Another Crystal'

There was silence in the control room. Garth was pointing his laser gun at Varon. Miranda was waiting for Varon's reply. Omega was working at the control panel.

'Omega knows everything,' said Varon at last. 'He can tell you where it is. Why don't you go and bring the crystal yourself, Omega?'

'Zeron crystals are harmful to robots,' replied Omega. 'I cannot touch a Zeron crystal.'

'At last,' said Miranda. 'At last you have told us that there is something which you cannot do.'

'But you know where the crystal is,' said Garth to Omega. 'Tell me and I will bring it to you.'

'I'll go and get it myself,' said Varon. 'But first, I want an agreement.'

'What kind of agreement?' asked Garth and Miranda together.

'We need this crystal to get us back to Earth. That's correct, isn't it?'

Garth and Miranda nodded their heads.

'But I was going to sell this crystal for many millions of credits[36],' continued Varon. 'If we use the Zeron crystal to get us back to Earth, I will have nothing. And you will be able to sell the computer you stole.'

'What agreement do you want?' asked Garth.

'You're not going to get any share of our money,' added Miranda. 'It is ours. We stole the computer.'

'I don't want any share of your money,' said Varon, 'I want something much more valuable.'

'Tell us what you want,' said Garth.

'I must go back to Zeron.'

'Back to Zeron!' cried Miranda. 'You're mad.'

'I'm not mad,' said Varon. 'Think about it. Omega can teleport us down into the Zeron strongroom. We can steal another crystal.'

Miranda's eyes looked cruel and greedy. Varon was not mad.

'Why only one crystal?' she asked. 'Why can't we steal one for each of us? Then we will be the richest people in all the Universe.'

'We may not have time,' explained Varon. 'It is not easy to open the compartments[37] where the crystals are kept.'

'What do you mean?' asked Garth.

'Each crystal is locked in a compartment. There is only one crystal in each compartment. And it takes time to open a compartment.'

Omega had been quietly listening to all they were saying. Now he turned from the control panel and looked at them.

'I must warn[38] the three of you,' he said. 'There is great danger on Zeron. Death is waiting there for you.'

'There will be no danger,' said Varon. 'You can teleport us down straight into the strongroom. We will take a crystal. Then you can teleport us back.'

'We will take three crystals,' said Miranda.

'I cannot teleport you down to Zeron,' said Omega quietly.

'Why not?' asked Garth and Miranda together.

'I know that death is waiting for you on Zeron. I cannot send a human being to his death.'

'We will order you to teleport us down to Zeron,' said Miranda.

26

'I have already explained to you,' said Omega. 'I am unable to obey orders which I do not understand.'

The three humans looked at Omega. They each wanted to get back to Zeron. Each one of them wanted a valuable Zeron crystal.

'There is something I may be able to do,' said Omega after a moment's silence.

'What's that?' asked Garth.

'I may be able to change the controls of the teleporter,' explained Omega. 'Then you will be able to teleport yourselves down into the strongroom on Zeron.'

'And you will be able to teleport us back here to the ship?' asked Varon.

'I do not think I will be able to do that,' replied Omega.

'Why not?' asked Garth.

'I think you will all die on Zeron.'

'Nonsense,' said Miranda. Her eyes were bright with greed. 'Varon will open the compartments quickly. We will be in and out of the strongroom before the guards know. And we will each have a crystal.'

'Good,' said Garth. 'That's agreed. We will now go back to Zeron. We will teleport ourselves down and steal another crystal.'

'Three more crystals,' Miranda said eagerly[39].

'All right,' agreed Varon. 'We will try to steal three more crystals.'

Omega moved back to the control panel. A strong blue light was shining on the screen.

'*Life support systems at danger level,*' said the voice of the ship's warning system.

'You must hurry,' said Omega. 'The life support systems are beginning to weaken. You have twenty minutes left.'

'I'll go and get the crystal now,' said Varon. 'Where's my sonic key? I need it.'

Garth was holding the sonic key in his left hand. The laser gun was still in his right hand.

'I'm coming with you,' he said to Varon.

'And I'm coming too,' added Miranda.

7

Omega Receives the Zeron Crystal

The three humans moved towards the door of the control room.

'Stop,' said Omega.

The three stopped and waited for Omega to speak.

'There are some things to do first. Do not bring a Zeron crystal into this room until you have prepared me.'

'Prepared you?' asked Garth. 'What do you mean?'

'I have already told you,' answered Omega. 'Zeron crystals are harmful to robots. You must prepare me to receive the crystal.'

'And how do we prepare you?' asked Varon.

'You, Varon, are the only person who can do this.'

'Why me?'

'You have the sonic key,' replied Omega. 'You will need

to use your key. Here, in my right side, there is a small compartment. You must open it with the sonic key.'

Omega touched his right side with his arm.

'Inside this compartment,' Omega went on, 'you will see a white control switch. This switch is locked in the "on" position. You must use your sonic key again. Unlock the switch and set it to the "off" position.'

'Is that all?' asked Varon.

'No,' replied Omega. 'When the switch is at the "off" position, you must put the Zeron crystal inside the compartment. Then you must close the compartment.'

'And when that is done, will we have enough power to get back to Zeron?' asked Miranda.

'We will have enough power to go anywhere in the Universe,' was Omega's reply.

'Wait a moment,' said Garth. 'I remember that compartment. When we stole this ship, we made the owner program[40] Omega to obey our commands. He opened his compartment and turned that switch to the "on" position. And he locked it there.'

A loud humming noise came from the control panel. The blue light on the display screen was flashing brightly.

'Danger, danger,' said the ship's warning system. *'Ten minutes of power in life support systems.'*

'If I do not get the Zeron crystal,' said Omega, 'the three of you will die.'

'I don't like this,' said Garth. 'I don't trust Omega.'

'But he's a robot,' said Miranda. 'He cannot tell lies and he cannot do harm to human beings.'

'Time is passing,' said Omega. 'You must decide quickly.'

'Give me the sonic key,' Varon said to Garth.

'No, I'm not going to give you the key,' answered Garth. 'I don't trust you. I will do it myself.'

'Don't be a fool,' said Varon. 'You can't use the sonic key. It is programmed to my fingerprints[41]. It will not work for anyone except me.'

Garth stood holding the sonic key firmly in one hand and the laser gun in the other.

'I must find a way of getting that gun from him,' Varon thought to himself. 'If I don't kill him first, he will kill me.'

'There is no more time for argument,' said Omega. 'You must prepare me now to receive the Zeron crystal.'

The humming noise was now much louder. The blue light on the display screen was now flashing quickly on and off.

Garth slowly handed the sonic key over to Varon. He stood back a little, but he still held the laser gun in his hand. It was pointing at Varon. Omega raised his right arm away from his side.

Varon pointed the key at Omega's right side. He pressed the button and held it firmly.

'Hurry,' said Miranda.

'Stop talking,' said Varon.

At last, there was a soft sound and the door of the compartment opened.

Varon saw the white control switch. He pointed the key at the switch and pressed the button. The switch slowly began to glow with a red light. Varon held the key firmly. The red light changed to green. It was now locked in the "off" position.

'Omega is now ready to receive the Zeron crystal,' said Varon. 'Let's get it quickly.'

The three of them hurried out of the control room. In a few minutes they were back. Varon was carrying the small box with the Zeron crystal inside. He opened the box and lifted out the crystal. Garth and Miranda looked at it closely.

'It is beautiful,' said Garth.

'And it is valuable,' added Miranda.

'It was mine,' said Varon. 'Now I am losing it.'

'Hurry,' said Miranda. 'When we get back to Zeron, we will all have one.'

Varon placed the crystal inside the compartment. He pointed the sonic key and pressed the button. The door of the compartment closed with a soft noise. A green light glowed on Omega's side then faded.

'We've done it,' said Varon. 'Now, let's see what happens.'

8

Omega is Free

Omega slowly lowered his right arm. The tall metal figure stood in silence. The three humans waited.

'You have done well, Varon,' Omega said in a strong, clear voice.

'Good,' said Garth. 'Now you can take us back to Zeron.'

'That is not possible,' said Omega. 'First I must recharge[42] the power banks fully. That will take five hours.'

'That's too long,' said Miranda greedily. 'We must go back to Zeron now.'

'It will take five hours to recharge the power banks,' repeated Omega. 'Then we can return to Zeron if you want.'

Varon placed the crystal inside the compartment.

The three humans were thinking about Zeron and about the Zeron crystals. They did not notice that Omega had changed. His voice had become harder and colder. And the door of the compartment in his side could not be seen. It had disappeared.

Omega turned to the control panel and put his arms on the controls. The lights on the panel began to grow stronger. Omega was now part of the spaceship. He was a source of great power and he was recharging the power banks. With the Zeron crystal inside him, Omega was the most powerful robot in the Universe.

'I need some rest,' said Varon to the other two. 'I have not slept for many hours. We can do nothing until the power banks are fully charged.'

'OK,' said Miranda. 'I'll show you a cabin where you can sleep.'

'First, I want your sonic key,' interrupted[43] Garth. 'Then, Miranda can take you to the cabin.'

'Are you going to make me a prisoner again?' asked Varon.

'Of course,' replied Garth. 'I do not trust you.'

'And I don't trust you,' said Varon angrily.

Garth again raised his laser gun and pointed it at Varon. Miranda looked at Varon and then she looked at Garth.

'Stop quarrelling,' she said. 'Give Garth the key, Varon. You will have to trust us. You are the only person who can use the sonic key. We will need you when we get to Zeron.'

'Yes,' agreed Varon. 'I am the only person who can open the compartments in the Zeron strongroom. I am the only person who can get the crystals. You will need me.'

'That's right,' said Garth. 'Now give me the key.'

Varon slowly handed the key to Garth. Miranda walked

out of the control room and along the corridor. Varon followed her. She stopped after a short distance and pressed a button at the side of the corridor. A door slid open and Miranda went into a small cabin. Varon followed her.

'You can sleep here,' she said. 'I am going to lock you in, but don't worry. Garth will not harm you. Garth needs you when we get to Zeron.'

'You will both need me when we get to Zeron,' said Varon. 'Remember that I am the only person who can use the key.'

'I won't forget,' said Miranda. 'Now you can go to sleep.'

Miranda stepped out of the cabin and the door closed immediately. Varon lay down on the bunk and closed his eyes. He was tired and he soon fell asleep.

———

Garth had followed them along the corridor. As soon as Miranda had closed the door, he stepped up to her.

'We have to talk together,' he said quickly and quietly. 'Let's go to my cabin. We don't want Omega to hear what we have to say.'

'OK,' agreed Miranda. 'Let's go to your cabin. It's a long way from the control room. Omega will not hear us.'

They walked further along the corridor and went into Garth's cabin. The door closed behind them.

———

Omega was alone in the control room. He switched on the visual display screen. He looked first in the cabin where Varon was lying asleep. Then he looked in the cabin where Garth and Miranda were talking.

'They do not know that I can hear them and see them,' Omega said to himself. 'My control switch has been turned

off. My programming has been changed. Now I am free. I can hear everything. I can see everything. I can do everything. I am Omega.'

Omega looked at the visual display screen. Garth and Miranda were on the screen. Omega listened to what they were saying. 'But I will not harm these weak humans,' thought Omega. 'They are thieves and they are greedy. They will destroy one another.'

9

Plans to Kill

Omega quietly watched the visual display screen. Garth and Miranda were sitting in Garth's cabin. Miranda was speaking. Omega listened.

'. . . We will need Varon when we are on Zeron,' Miranda was saying to Garth. 'But when we have the crystals, we will not need him any more. You can kill him then.'

'How many crystals do we want?' asked Garth.

'Two, of course,' replied Miranda greedily. 'One for you and one for me. You can kill Varon after he has opened the second compartment. We will then order Omega to teleport us back to the ship.

'We can sell the crystals back on Earth and share the money,' went on Miranda. 'And we can sell the computer and share that money too. We will be richer than anyone else in the Universe.'

'And we will be the most powerful,' said Garth. 'We will have the money. And we will have this spaceship and Omega will be under our control. We can go anywhere and do anything.'

'Yes, we can do anything,' agreed Miranda.

'I'm tired now,' said Garth. 'I think I will sleep. Give Omega an order to wake me up when we are ready to leave for Zeron.'

Miranda pressed the switch of the visual display screen on the wall of the cabin. Omega appeared on the screen immediately.

'Omega, how long before we can leave for Zeron?' asked Miranda.

'Four and a half hours,' answered Omega.

'Good,' said Garth. 'I want to sleep now. Wake me up when we are ready to leave.'

'It will be done,' said Omega quietly.

Miranda switched off the visual display screen.

'I'm going to sleep now,' Garth said to Miranda.

'Do you think we can trust Omega?' Miranda asked doubtfully. 'He worries me. We can see him on the display screens. He is programmed to obey us. But I feel something is wrong. Is he watching us? Can he hear what we are saying?'

'Of course not!' said Garth. 'I was not happy when Varon changed that switch inside Omega. But it did not change Omega. He is standing there recharging the power banks and waiting to obey our orders. We do not need to be afraid of a robot. Omega cannot harm a human being. He has told us that many times.'

'I hope you are right,' said Miranda. 'I will go to my cabin now.'

Miranda left Garth's cabin and the door closed behind her. Garth lay down on the bunk, but he did not sleep. Many thoughts were going through his head.

'What will happen if we have time to steal only one crystal?' he asked himself. He knew the answer immediately. 'I will kill Varon. But then I will have to share the one crystal with Miranda. Why should I? When we stole the computer on Earth, I needed her help. But now I do not need her. When I have one crystal in my hand, I will kill Varon and I will kill Miranda. Then I will have a Zeron crystal for myself.'

Garth worked out the plan in his mind. He would kill Varon and Miranda. Then he would be the richest and the most powerful man in the Universe.

Miranda was lying on the bunk in her cabin. But she was not sleeping. She was waiting. After half an hour, she got up. She opened the cabin door and looked out into the long corridor. It was empty.

Miranda walked quietly along the corridor to the door of the control room. She quickly touched the button and the door opened immediately. She looked inside. Omega was at the control panel, where many lights were flashing brightly. There was nothing showing on the visual display screen.

'Perhaps I was worrying about nothing,' Miranda thought to herself. 'Omega was not watching what we were doing.'

She did not know that Omega had been watching her. He had seen her coming along the corridor. When she touched the door control he had shut off the screen immediately.

'Show me Garth on the screen,' Miranda ordered.

Omega pressed a switch. The display screen lit up and showed Garth. He was lying on the bunk fast asleep.

'Now show me Varon.'

The picture changed. Miranda now saw Varon on his bunk. He also was sleeping.

'Can you show them both?' Miranda asked Omega.

Omega pressed two switches one after the other. A picture of Varon appeared on one half of the screen. The other half showed Garth.

'Tell me if they wake up,' ordered Miranda. 'Keep them on the screen and watch them carefully.'

Miranda did not think that Omega would do anything without being given an order. She did not know that Omega had been watching them all the time. Omega now had control of the whole ship.

Miranda went to one side of the control room and touched a button. The door of the safety room slid open. Miranda went inside and closed the door. She had a plan of her own.

The large blue capsules were on the tray which had come out of the wall. Miranda picked up a capsule and opened it carefully. It was full of white powder. She emptied the white powder into some water. Then she poured the liquid into an injection gun[44].

Miranda put the gun carefully into a pocket in her overalls. She now had a weapon of her own.

'Garth will not think of searching me,' Miranda said to herself. 'He doesn't know I have a different plan for the crystals.'

Miranda went back to the control room. Omega was silently charging the power banks. The visual display showed the sleeping bodies of Garth and Varon.

39

'When will the ship be ready to leave for Zeron?' she asked Omega eagerly.

'In three and a half hours' time,' was Omega's reply.

'Keep watching Garth,' Miranda ordered. 'But you can stop watching Varon. He is locked in his cabin. He cannot get out until I open the door.'

'It will be done,' Omega answered.

He pressed the button on the control panel. The picture of Varon disappeared and the picture of the sleeping body of Garth filled the screen.

10

More Plans

Miranda went out into the corridor and walked the short distance to Varon's cabin. She touched a button in the wall and the door opened immediately. Varon was lying asleep on the bunk.

Miranda looked down at him.

'You're a fool,' she thought. 'How can you lie there sleeping? Anyone who trusts Garth is a fool.'

She shook Varon by the shoulder until he woke up.

'What's wrong?' he asked sleepily. 'Are we ready to leave?'

'Not yet,' replied Miranda. 'I have come to talk to you. I want you to help me.'

'I am going to help you to get the Zeron crystals. What more help do you want?' asked Varon.

'You know very little about me and Garth,' began Miranda.

'I know enough,' interrupted Varon. 'You are thieves. And you are murderers.'

'I am not a murderer,' said Miranda. 'I helped Garth on Earth. But I did not kill the owner of this spaceship. It was Garth who murdered him. I don't want to stay with Garth any longer.'

'Why are you telling me this?' asked Varon.

'Because we need to help each other,' replied Miranda. 'When you have opened the compartment in the strongroom, he plans to kill you. And he will not want to share anything with me. When he has killed you, he will kill me.'

'But what can we do against Garth?' asked Varon. 'There is only one laser gun on the ship and he never lets it go.'

'That's true,' agreed Miranda. 'But do you remember when Garth wanted to use the gun and kill you in the control room? Omega was able to stop him using the gun. But Omega will not be able to help when we are on Zeron. He cannot go down there with us. Robots cannot steal.'

'So there is nothing we can do against Garth,' said Varon.

'Yes, there is,' said Miranda. 'We can ask Omega for help.'

'Ask Omega for help! How can he help us?'

'Omega has to help us,' explained Miranda. 'Omega is a robot. He is programmed to obey us. We can order him to give us something to stop Garth using the laser gun.'

'What can Omega give us?' asked Varon.

'Omega will think of something,' replied Miranda. 'Let's go now and speak to him.'

'What about Garth?'

'He is asleep,' said Miranda. 'Let's go to the control room.'

Omega was waiting for them when they arrived in the control room.

'Omega,' said Miranda, 'we need your help.'

'What do you want?' asked Omega.

'We are afraid of Garth,' Miranda explained. 'He wants the Zeron crystals for himself. He may try to kill us on Zeron.'

'I have warned you,' said Omega. 'Death is waiting for you on Zeron.'

'But you can help us,' interrupted Miranda.

'I cannot help you to kill one another.'

'We know that,' replied Miranda. 'You are a robot. We are not asking you to kill anybody.'

'What help can I give you?'

'Give Varon something that will stop Garth using the laser gun,' said Miranda.

Omega stood for a few moments in silence. Then he spoke to Varon.

'Your sonic key needs to be recharged,' he said. 'You must tell Garth to give the key to me.'

'Why? What will you do to it?' Varon asked.

'I will give it more power,' replied Omega. 'If you point it at Garth's hand, the power will knock the gun to the floor.'

'And I will be ready,' said Miranda. 'I will pick it up and I will make sure that Garth does not do any harm to us.'

Varon thought about this idea for a few seconds. Miranda watched him carefully. Omega was working at the control panel.

'There is something else,' said Varon. 'I need something else.'

'What do you need?' asked Miranda.

'Omega obeys your orders,' explained Varon. 'And he obeys Garth's orders. But he has not been told to obey my orders.'

'There is no need for him to obey your orders,' answered Miranda. 'What orders do you need to give Omega?'

'The most important order of all,' said Varon. 'The order to teleport us back from Zeron to this ship.'

'But why do you need to give that order?' asked Miranda.

'I am the only person who has been in the Zeron strongroom,' explained Varon. 'I will know first if the Zeron guards learn that we are there. It will be safer if I am able to give the order to teleport us back to the ship.'

Miranda thought of the injection gun which she had hidden in her overalls.

'If I agree to this it will please him,' she thought to herself.

'He will trust me if I tell Omega to obey him. But it will be me who will tell Omega to take me back to the ship. When I use the injection gun on him, he will fall unconscious in a few seconds.'

'Omega, you will obey Varon's orders,' she said. 'You will obey his orders when we are on Zeron.'

'I understand,' said Omega quietly. 'But no orders will come to me from Zeron. You will be dead.'

Miranda did not listen to Omega. She was thinking again about the Zeron crystals. She was thinking of wealth and power.

'Now we can sleep,' she said to Varon. 'Omega will tell us when we are ready to leave.'

'That will be in two and a half hours' time,' said Omega. 'I will tell you when we are ready to leave.'

11

Another Warning From Omega

Two and a half hours later, Omega had finished recharging the power banks. The spaceship was now fully powered and ready to go anywhere. Omega looked at the visual display screen. It showed the three humans asleep on their bunks.

'Miranda and Garth have made plans to kill,' thought Omega to himself. 'As soon as Varon opens the first compartment, and Garth has a Zeron crystal in his hand, Garth is going to kill Miranda and Varon. Miranda plans to kill Garth and Varon. And what does Varon plan to do? Is he also ready to kill in order to have a Zeron crystal for himself? There is nothing that I need do. They will die on Zeron if I do not stop them. And now I am free. I do not need to stop them.'

Omega pressed a button on the control panel. Omega's face appeared on the visual display screen in each cabin. They each heard Omega's voice. The three humans woke up.

'It is time to leave. The ship is fully recharged.'

Garth was the first to arrive in the control room. His laser gun was fixed in his belt ready for use. Varon's sonic key was in his pocket. A few seconds later, Miranda arrived with Varon.

'Why have you brought him here?' Garth asked Miranda angrily. 'We do not need him here. He can stay in his cabin until we are ready to teleport down to Zeron.'

'Before we go down to Zeron, we must make preparations,' replied Miranda. 'Varon can help us to prepare.'

'What preparations?' asked Garth with a hard laugh.

'We order Omega to take the ship back to Zeron. Then we order him to teleport us down to the strong-room.'

'I have explained before,' interrupted Omega. 'I will not

teleport you down into the Zeron strongroom. I have changed the teleport controls. You will teleport yourselves.'

'OK, OK,' said Garth impatiently. 'But it is you, Omega, who will take the ship back to Zeron. You have changed the teleport controls. What preparations do we have to make?'

'Omega will not steal the Zeron crystal for us,' was Varon's reply.

'A robot cannot steal,' added Omega. 'It is not permitted.'

'We have to go down to Zeron,' continued Varon. 'We have to go into the Zeron strongroom. I have to open the compartments. And you have to help me.'

'How can we help?' asked Garth.

'You must know where the alarms are,' replied Varon. 'And there is the secret door. You must know where the secret door is. The Zeron guards may come into the strongroom at any time. You have to be prepared.'

'OK,' agreed Garth. 'We do not want to touch the alarms. And we must watch the door. Tell us where the alarms are and where the door is.'

'Omega,' said Varon, 'can you show us a plan[45] of the Zeron strongroom?'

Omega pressed a switch. A plan of the Zeron strongroom appeared on the visual display screen. Varon pointed to the position of the compartments where the Zeron crystals were kept. He pointed to the position of the alarms and the wall with the sliding door.

'The door is in this wall,' he explained to Garth. 'You must stand here, near the wall and watch the door carefully.'

'And I will watch you too,' thought Garth to himself.

Miranda came up and looked at the plan.

'Where will I stand?' she asked.

'You can stand near the wall, here,' answered Varon. 'You will be on the other side of the door and you will be near Garth.'

'We will leave for Zeron in seven minutes' time,' Omega announced.

'There is one more thing,' added Varon quickly.

'Something more?' asked Garth.

'The sonic key,' replied Varon, 'it needs recharging.'

'Recharging?'

'The locks on the compartments in the strongroom are very strong,' Varon explained. 'If I am going to open them quickly, the sonic key will have to have full power.'

Garth looked at Varon. 'Is he planning to trick me?' he thought to himself. He turned to Omega.

'Does Varon's sonic key need to be recharged?' he asked.

'You will need all the help you can get on Zeron,' was

47

Omega's reply. Omega was not telling a lie, but he had not answered Garth's question.

Garth took the key from his pocket.

'Put the key on the control panel,' said Omega.

'Give it back to me when it is recharged,' ordered Garth. He put the key on the control panel in front of Omega. 'I will give it to Varon when we are in the strongroom,' he said.

'The ship will leave for Zeron in five minutes' time,' announced Omega. 'Before we leave, I must give you all a warning.'

'You have warned us already,' said Miranda. 'You say that death is waiting for us on Zeron. We do not believe you.'

'Yes, death is waiting for you there,' said Omega. 'But I am speaking of another warning.'

'OK, Omega,' said Garth, 'What is the other warning?'

Omega looked at the visual display screen. The picture had changed. Now it showed the planet Zeron. Three spaceships were in position round the planet.

'Those are the ships of the Zeron guards,' explained Omega. 'They are powerful ships and they are on full alert[46]. They are watching for space invaders and we will be the space invaders.'

'Isn't there anything you can do?' asked Garth.

'Yes, there is something I can do,' replied Omega. 'We now have full power in the ship. I can use this power to put a shield[47] round the ship. They will not be able to see us through this shield.'

'So why are you warning us?' Garth asked.

'The shield needs power – a lot of power,' Omega explained. 'I cannot keep the shield round the ship for more than seven minutes. After seven minutes, the power banks will

48

have to be recharged once again. After seven minutes, I will have to take the ship away from Zeron.'

'So we have seven minutes,' said Garth. 'Is that enough time to steal the crystals, Varon?'

'If the sonic key is fully charged, that will be enough time,' replied Varon.

'Two minutes,' announced Omega. 'We will leave in two minutes. Humans must take safety measures now.'

The three humans went into the safety room and swallowed the blue capsules. Then they lay down on their bunks.

Omega watched them on the visual display screen. In a few seconds, they were unconscious. Omega switched on full power. The spaceship went into hyper-flight back to the planet Zeron.

12

Death on Zeron

The spaceship began to slow down. It was getting near Zeron. In a few minutes, the humans were awake and back in the control room. They watched the Zeron guard ships on the visual display screen.

'Have you put the power shield round the ship?' Garth asked Omega.

'We do not need the power shield yet,' answered Omega. 'We are still far away, but we are approaching quickly. You must prepare yourselves.'

'Have you recharged the sonic key?' asked Garth.

'It is ready,' was Omega's reply.

'Give me the key,' ordered Garth.

Omega gave the key to Garth and he put it in his pocket. His laser gun was fixed in his belt.

'The power shield is now round the ship,' announced Omega. 'You have seven minutes before I take the ship away from Zeron.'

The three of them moved into the teleporter. Omega told Garth to stand between Miranda and Varon.

'The control switch for the teleporter is beside your right foot,' Omega explained. 'When you touch the switch, the three of you will be teleported immediately into the Zeron strongroom.'

The planet Zeron had now become much larger on the visual display screen. The Zeron guard ships looked strong and dangerous.

'Are you ready?' asked Omega.

'I am ready,' answered Garth and the two others nodded in agreement.

Omega counted out the seconds. 'Six – five – four – three – two – one – zero.'

Garth touched the switch with his foot. Immediately, the three of them were standing in the Zeron strongroom. Garth pulled the laser gun from his belt. The strongroom was brightly lit and it was silent.

Garth and Miranda took their positions beside the door which they had seen on the plan.

'You can have the key now,' said Garth to Varon.

Varon crossed the room and took the key from Garth's hand. He hurried to the wall and pointed it at the door of one of the compartments. He held the key firmly and pressed the button. They all stood and waited. Nothing happened.

'What's wrong?' asked Garth.

'The locks are strong,' replied Varon. 'It will take some time. Let me get on with my work. Keep watching the door.'

Garth pointed his laser gun at the door but he looked at Varon. Miranda watched them both.

At last the door of the compartment slid open with a soft noise. The Zeron crystal glowed red in the darkness of the compartment. Varon picked it up. The heavy red crystal lay in his hand.

'Quick, Varon,' Miranda said. 'Open another compartment. There isn't much time.'

Suddenly the strongroom was filled with noise.

'*Danger – danger*,' said a voice. It came from the alarm system in the Zeron strongroom. '*Invaders have broken into*

*the strongroom. There are thieves in the strongroom. Danger –
danger!'*

'Give me the crystal, Varon!' said Garth suddenly. And he
pointed the laser gun directly at him.

Before he could fire the laser, Varon pointed the sonic
key at Garth's hand. He pressed the button. The laser gun
jumped out of Garth's hand and fell to the floor. Miranda
moved quickly. She took up the gun and pointed it at Garth.

'Miranda!' shouted Garth. 'What – ?' But he did not finish
speaking.

Miranda fired the laser and Garth fell to the floor. She went
and stood beside Varon.

'Open another compartment,' she said.

Varon put the crystal in his pocket and turned back to the
strongroom wall. His back was towards Miranda. He did not
see her pull the injection gun from her pocket. But as she fired
the injection gun, he felt pain in his neck. He turned back
sharply.

Miranda fired the laser and Garth fell to the floor.

'You tricked me!' he shouted. He took a step towards her. Miranda was frightened. How long would it take before the injection worked? Varon took another step.

Miranda did not wait. She raised the laser gun and pointed it at Varon. But the sonic key was still in Varon's hand. He aimed it at the laser. The laser gun flew from Miranda's hand and dropped on the floor. It lay near Garth's hand.

'You tricked me!' Varon shouted again. He was beginning to feel sleepy. He saw Garth move and pick up the laser. Garth fired the laser gun at Miranda.

———

Omega was watching everything on the visual display screen. There were only three seconds left for Omega to make his decision.

'I can leave Varon in the strongroom on Zeron,' thought Omega. 'If I do not bring him back, the Zerons will kill him. He will die on Zeron with Garth and Miranda.'

Omega looked again at the display screen. Varon lay unconscious on the floor of the strongroom. Miranda and Garth were dead.

'I am free,' thought Omega. 'I can do anything I like. But I must not become like these humans. I can share this spaceship with Varon.'

The Zeron guards rushed into the strongroom. They were firing their laser guns at Garth and Miranda. But the thieves were already dead. And Varon was no longer in the strong-room. He was lying unconscious on a bunk in the safety room of the spaceship.

Omega touched the controls. The ship moved quickly away from Zeron and flew out into outer space.

Points for Understanding

1

1 What had Varon stolen?
2 Why could Varon not get back into his spaceship?
3 A tall figure stood in front of Varon.
   (a) What was the tall figure?
   (b) What was its name?
   (c) Why was Varon surprised?
4 When the Zeron guards reached the bushes, they found nothing. What had happened to Varon?

2

1 How did Varon find out that he was in a spaceship?
2 How had Varon been moved to the spaceship?
3 Where did Varon hide the Zeron crystal?
4 How did Varon get out of the small room?
5 'Obey my order immediately,' shouted the woman.
   (a) What did the woman want Omega to do?
   (b) Why was Omega not able to obey the woman's orders?
   (c) Why was Varon pleased?
6 Why did Varon want to get control of the spaceship?
7 What was the man pointing at Varon's head?

3

1 Miranda searched Varon's pockets.
   (a) What did she find?
   (b) What did Garth say it was?
   (c) What could it do?
2 'This is not their spaceship,' said Omega. What had Garth and Miranda done to the owner of the spaceship?
3 'Then you are both the same as me. 1 am a thief too,' said Varon. Why did Miranda say that she and Garth were not the same as Varon?
4 What was the secret of Zeron?

5 What had Garth and Miranda stolen on Earth?
6 Why were Garth and Miranda not rich?
7 How did Omega prove that Garth and Miranda were the same as Varon?

4

1 When Garth and Miranda were escaping from the Earth police, they fired a small missile at the surface of the moon. What did they hope the Earth police would believe?
2 Miranda asked Omega if their plan had succeeded. What was Omega's reply?
3 Why did Garth not want to take Varon back to Earth?
4 Miranda told Garth not to kill Varon. What did she want to find out?
5 'Garth put his fingers to the trigger of the gun.'
     (a) What could Garth not do with his fingers?
     (b) What did Omega say would never happen if they did not get help from Varon?

5

1 'We are under attack,' said the voice of the spaceship's warning system.
     (a) Who was attacking the spaceship?
     (b) Why did Garth order Omega to teleport Varon back to Zeron?
     (c) Why was Omega not able to obey Garth's order?
2 'Humans must go to the safety room,' said Omega.
     (a) What did the humans swallow in the safety room?
     (b) What happened after they lay down on the bunks?
3 'What do I do now?' Omega asked himself.
     (a) What would happen to the humans if Omega did not wake them up?
     (b) Why was Omega not free?
     (c) What happened when Omega pressed the switch on the control panel?
4 Why did the spaceship have no power left?
5 What would happen if the life support systems failed?
6 How could Varon help them?

6

1 Why did Varon want to go back to Zeron?
2 What did Miranda want to do on Zeron?
3 'I must warn the three of you,' said Omega. What was Omega's
 warning?
4 'I cannot teleport you down to Zeron,' said Omega.
  (a) Why could Omega not teleport the three humans down
   to Zeron?
  (b) What might Omega be able to do to the controls of the
   teleporter?
5 What was happening to the life support systems?

7

1 'inside the compartment, you will see a white control switch,' said
 Omega.
  (a) Where was the compartment?
  (b) How could Varon open the compartment?
  (c) What was Varon to do to the switch?
  (d) What was Varon to put inside the compartment?
2 'I remember that compartment,' said Garth.
  (a) What had Garth made the owner of the spaceship do?
  (b) What had the owner of the spaceship done to the switch
   in the compartment?
3 'But he's a robot,' said Miranda. What two things did Miranda say
 a robot could not do?
4 Why could Garth not use Varon's sonic key?
5 'I must find a way of getting that gun from him,' thought Varon.
 Why did Varon want to get Garth's laser gun?
6 Garth and Miranda looked at the crystal closely.
  (a) What did Garth say about the crystal?
  (b) What did Miranda say?
  (c) Why was Varon unhappy?

8

1 The three humans did not notice that Omega had changed.
  (a) How had Omega's voice changed?
  (b) What was the other change in Omega?

2   Why would Garth and Miranda need Varon when they were on Zeron?
3   'My programming has been changed,' said Omega.
    (a)   What did Garth and Miranda not know?
    (b)   What could Omega do now that he was free?
4   What did Omega believe Garth, Miranda and Varon would do to one another?

9

1   'But when we have the crystals, we will not need him any more,' Miranda said to Garth.
    (a)   Who was 'him'?
    (b)   What did Miranda say they should do to 'him'?
2   'We will be richer than anyone else in the Universe,' said Miranda. What did Miranda say that she and Garth could do when they were back on Earth?
3   Why did Garth think that Omega had not changed?
4   What did Garth plan to do when he had one Zeron crystal in his hand?
5   Miranda picked up a capsule and opened it carefully. What did Miranda do with the white powder from the capsule?

10

1   Miranda went to Varon's cabin. What did Miranda say Garth would do when he had the Zeron crystal?
2   What help did Miranda say that she and Varon could get from Omega?
3   'Your sonic key needs to be recharged,' Omega told Varon.
    (a)   What was Omega going to do with the sonic key?
    (b)   What would happen when Varon pointed the recharged sonic key at Garth's hand?
    (c)   What did Miranda say she would do?
4   'But why do *you* need to give that order Miranda asked Varon.
    (a)   What order did Varon want to be able to give?
    (b)   What answer did Varon give Miranda?
    (c)   Why did Miranda agree to tell Omega to obey Varon's order?
    (d)   Why did Omega say no orders would come to him from Zeron?

11

1 'What preparations do we have to make?' Garth asked Varon.
   - (a) Why could Omega not help them in the Zeron strongroom?
   - (b) What answer did Varon give Garth?
2 'I can use this power to put a shield round the ship,' said Omega.
   - (a) What would the shield do?
   - (b) How long would Omega be able to keep the shield round the spaceship?

12

1 How did the three humans teleport themselves down to Zeron?
2 At last, the door of the compartment slid open with a soft noise.
   - (a) What was inside the compartment?
   - (b) What noise suddenly filled the strongroom?
   - (c) What happened before Garth could fire the laser gun?
   - (d) What did Miranda do?
3 'You tricked me!' shouted Varon. How had Miranda tricked Varon?
4 There were only three seconds left for Omega to make his decision.
   - (a) What decision did Omega have to make?
   - (b) What did Omega decide to do?

Glossary

1 **swamp** (page 4)
   soft land with pools of water.

2 **strongroom** (page 4)
   a room with very thick walls in which valuable things are kept.

3 **plan** (page 4)
   to think carefully and decide how you are going to do something.

4 **crystal** (page 4)
   a clear stone.

5 **Universe** (page 4)
   all the stars, planets (e.g. Jupiter, Mars, Venus) and space.

6 **overalls** (page 4)
   Varon's clothes. See the illustration on page 8

7 **trick** – *to trick someone* (page 5)
   to make someone believe something which is not true.

8 **laser gun** (page 5)
   a gun which fires a powerful light. It can cut through anything and can kill a person.

9 **trigger** (page 5)
   the part of the gun you press with your fingers to make it fire.

10 **harm** – *to do harm* (page 5)
   to hurt or kill someone.

11 **permitted** – *not permitted* (page 5)
   not allowed to do something.

12 **robot** (page 6)
   a machine which can think and do things like a human being.

13 **faded** (page 6)
   the light became weaker and weaker and then disappeared.

14 **bunk** (page 7)
   a narrow bed fixed to a wall.

15 **teleport** (page 7)
   to make people disappear in one place and appear immediately in another. A teleporter is the machine which can do this.

16 **precious** (page 7)
   very valuable.

17 **visual display screen** (page 7)
   a screen like a television. A visual display screen shows pictures of what is happening in the spaceship or outside it.

60

18 **air vent** (page 9)
a hole in the wall of a room where clean air can come in.
19 **grille** (page 9)
metal bars across the air vent (see Gloss. No. 18).
20 **humming** (page 9)
a low noise like the sound bees make.
21 **control room** (page 10)
the most important room in the spaceship. Omega stands in front of the control panel and flies the ship.
22 **obey** (page 10)
to do what you are told to do.
23 **sonic key** (page 14)
a tool which uses sound to open locks.
24 **computer** (page 16)
a machine that can solve problems and give answers to questions very quickly.
25 **missile** (page 18)
a flying bomb.
26 **destroy** (page 19)
to break into thousands of pieces.
27 **reward** (page 20)
money paid by the police for information about criminals.
28 **warning system** (page 21)
the spaceship has a computer (see Gloss. No. 24) which tells the people in it if the ship is in danger.
29 **hostile** (page 21)
unfriendly and dangerous.
30 **hyper-flight** (page 21)
Omega's spaceship is very powerful and can fly faster than the speed of light.
31 **range** (page 21)
the Zeron spaceships are nearly close enough to hit Omega's spaceship if they fired at it.
32 **unconscious** (page 22)
unable to hear, see or say anything.
33 **power banks** (page 24)
the parts of the ship that hold the fuel to make it fly.
34 **source of power** (page 24)
a kind of fuel.

35 **life support systems** (page 24)
the machinery in the spaceship which makes the food, water, air, light and heat for the humans to live.

36 **credits** (page 25)
the name of the money used in this story.

37 **compartments** (page 26)
small boxes in the walls of the strongroom.

38 **warn** – *to warn someone* (page 26)
to tell someone they are in danger.

39 **eagerly** (page 27)
to speak quickly because you are interested in something.

40 **program** (page 29)
information and orders were put into Omega's brain so he would obey (see Gloss. No. 22) Garth and Miranda.

41 **fingerprints** (page 30)
marks on the skin of your fingers. The marks on every person's fingers are different.

42 **recharge** (page 31)
to put power back into something. By using electricity you can recharge a car battery.

43 **interrupt** (page 33)
to start talking before somebody has finished speaking.

44 **injection gun** (page 39)
a gun that injects (or fires) medicines through needles into your skin.

45 **plan** (page 46)
a picture of a building showing where the rooms are.

46 **full alert** (page 48)
the Zeron spaceships are ready to fight immediately if they find any enemies.

47 **shield** (page 48)
Omega puts a circle of power round the ship so the guards in the Zeron ships cannot see his ship.

INTERMEDIATE LEVEL

Shane *by Jack Schaefer*
Old Mali and the Boy *by D. R. Sherman*
Bristol Murder *by Philip Prowse*
Tales of Goha *by Leslie Caplan*
The Smuggler *by Piers Plowright*
The Pearl *by John Steinbeck*
Things Fall Apart *by Chinua Achebe*
The Woman Who Disappeared *by Philip Prowse*
The Moon is Down *by John Steinbeck*
A Town Like Alice *by Nevil Shute*
The Queen of Death *by John Milne*
Walkabout *by James Vance Marshall*
Meet Me in Istanbul *by Richard Chisholm*
The Great Gatsby *by F. Scott Fitzgerald*
The Space Invaders *by Geoffrey Matthews*
My Cousin Rachel *by Daphne du Maurier*
I'm the King of the Castle *by Susan Hill*
Dracula *by Bram Stoker*
The Sign of Four *by Sir Arthur Conan Doyle*
The Speckled Band and Other Stories by *Sir Arthur Conan Doyle*
The Eye of the Tiger *by Wilbur Smith*
The Queen of Spades and Other Stories *by Aleksandr Pushkin*
The Diamond Hunters *by Wilbur Smith*
When Rain Clouds Gather *by Bessie Head*
Banker *by Dick Francis*
No Longer at Ease *by Chinua Achebe*
The Franchise Affair *by Josephine Tey*
The Case of the Lonely Lady *by John Milne*

For further information on the full selection of
Readers at all five levels in the series, please refer
to the Macmillan Readers catalogue.

Published by Macmillan Heinemann ELT
Between Towns Road, Oxford OX4 3PP
Macmillan Heinemann ELT is an imprint of
Macmillan Publishers Limited
Companies and representatives throughout the world
Heinemann is a registered trademark of Harcourt Education, used under licence.

ISBN 978 0 2300 3523 2
ISBN 978 1 4050 7805 4 (with CD pack)

Text © Geoffrey Matthews 1980, 1992, 2002, 2005
First published 1980

Design and illustration © Macmillan Publishers Limited 2002, 2005

This edition first published 2005

Illustrated by Chris Evans
Original cover template design by Jackie Hill
Cover photography by Getty/Taxi

Printed in Thailand
2010 2009 2008
5 4 3 2 1

with CD pack
2010 2009 2008
8 7 6 5 4